I Spy Diwali Book For Kids

How To Play

Try to answer the question
Turn the page to find the answer.
GOOD LUCK!

I Spy With My Little Eye Something Beginning With ...

A

It's An Apple

I Spy With My Little Eye
Something Beginning With ...

B

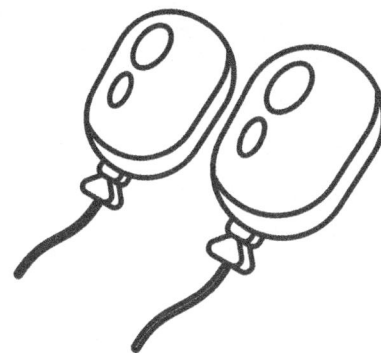

It's An Balloons

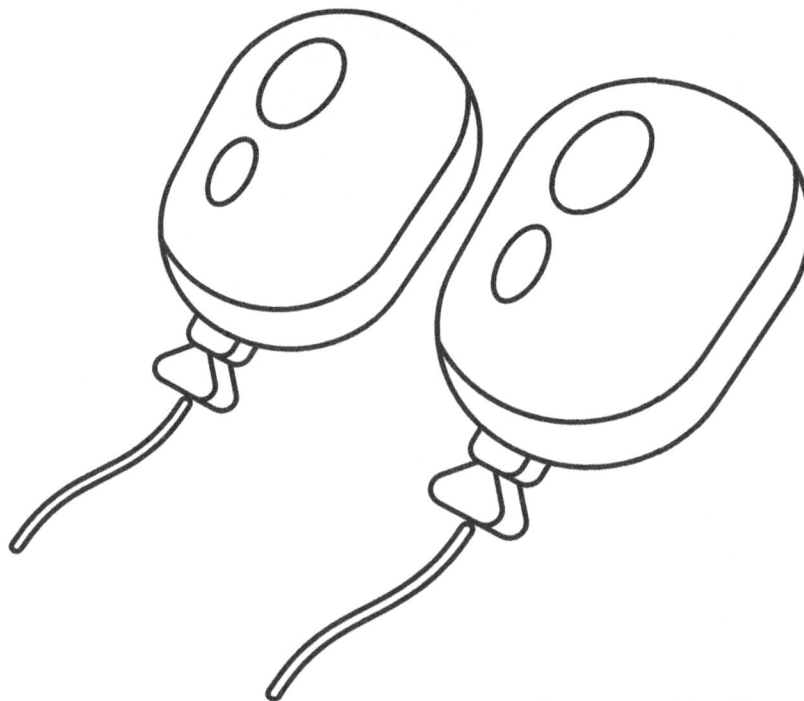

I Spy With My Little Eye
Something Beginning With ...

C

It's An Candy

I Spy With My Little Eye Something Beginning With ...

D

It's An
Diva Lamp

I Spy With My Little Eye Something Beginning With ...

It's An eagle

I Spy With My Little Eye Something Beginning With ...

 **F**

It's An Fireworks

I Spy With My Little Eye Something Beginning With ...

G

It's An Ganesha

I Spy With My Little Eye Something Beginning With ...

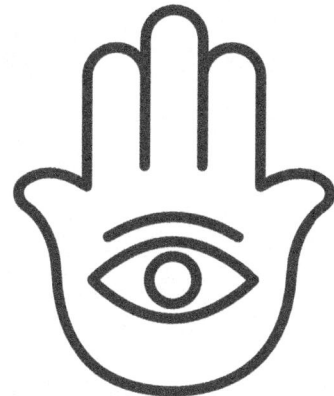

H

It's An Hamsa

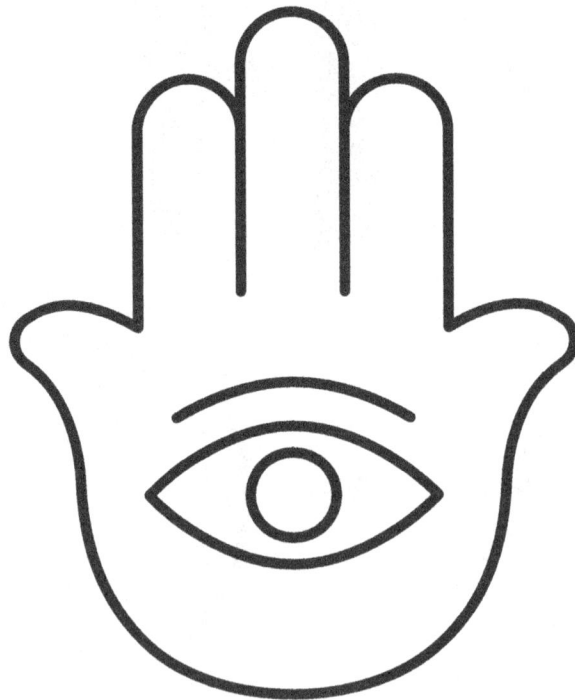

I Spy With My Little Eye Something Beginning With ...

It's An Indian flag

I Spy With My Little Eye Something Beginning With ...

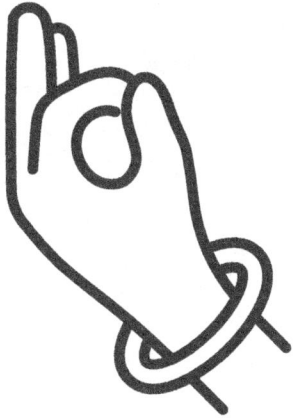

It's An Jewelery

I Spy With My Little Eye Something Beginning With ...

It's An krishna

I Spy With My Little Eye
Something Beginning With ...

It's An Lotus

I Spy With My Little Eye Something Beginning With ...

M

It's An Mehndi

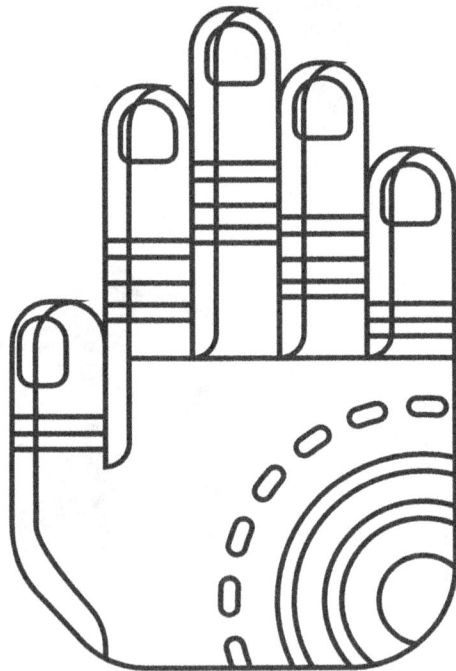

I Spy With My Little Eye Something Beginning With ...

N

It's An Necklace

I Spy With My Little Eye Something Beginning With ...

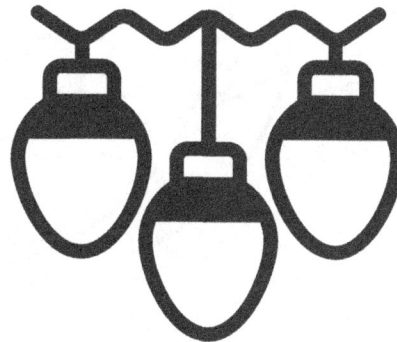

O

It's An Oil Lamp

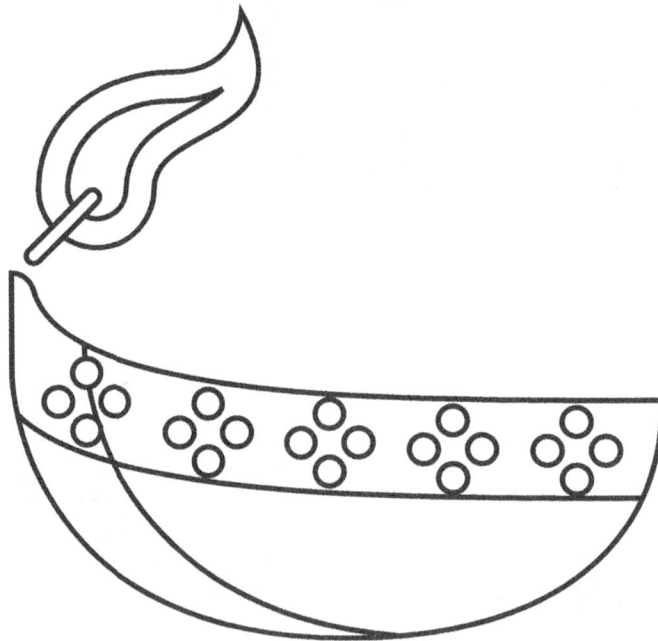

I Spy With My Little Eye Something Beginning With ...

P

It's An Presents

I Spy With My Little Eye Something Beginning With ...

Q

It's An Queen

I Spy With My Little Eye Something Beginning With ...

R

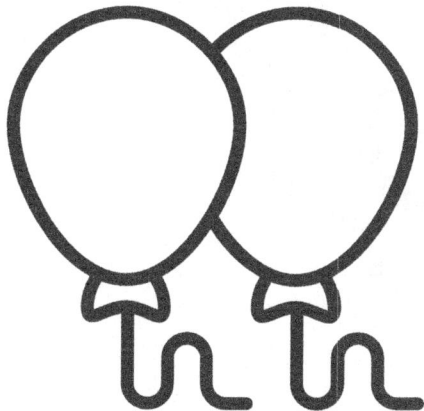

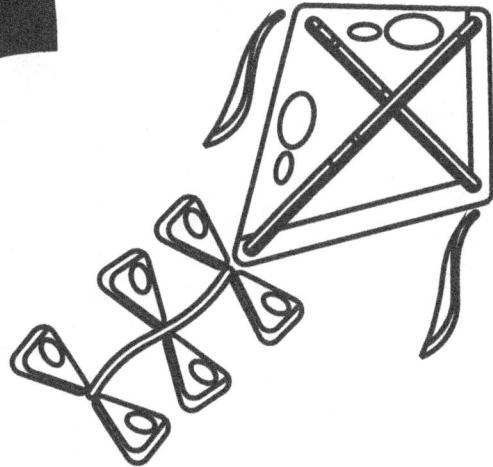

It's An
Rangoli pattern

I Spy With My Little Eye Something Beginning With ...

S

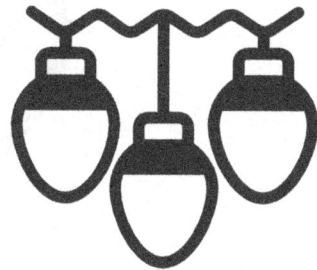

It's An Sitar

I Spy With My Little Eye Something Beginning With ...

T

It's An Tabla

I Spy With My Little Eye Something Beginning With ...

U

It's An Unicorn

I Spy With My Little Eye Something Beginning With ...

It's An Vedas Book

I Spy With My Little Eye Something Beginning With ...

It's An Whale

I Spy With My Little Eye
Something Beginning With ...

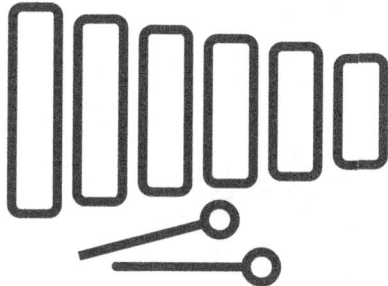

It's An Xylophone

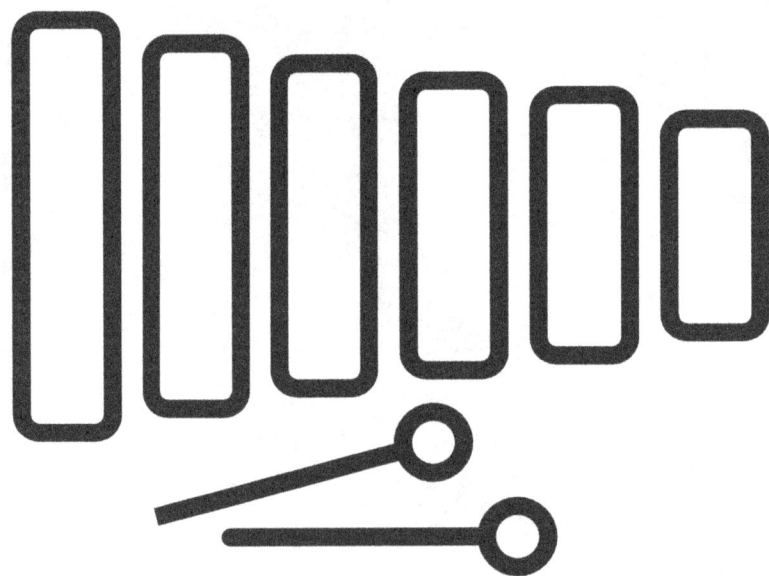

I Spy With My Little Eye Something Beginning With ...

It's An Yoga

I Spy With My Little Eye Something Beginning With ...

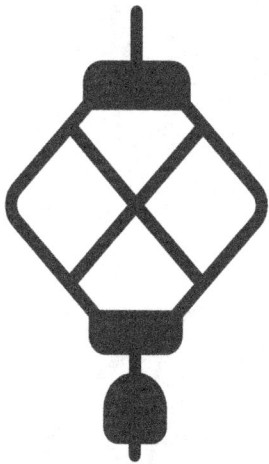

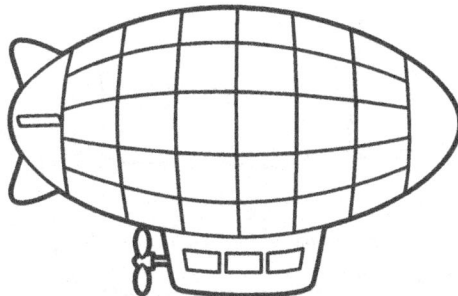

It's An Zeppelin

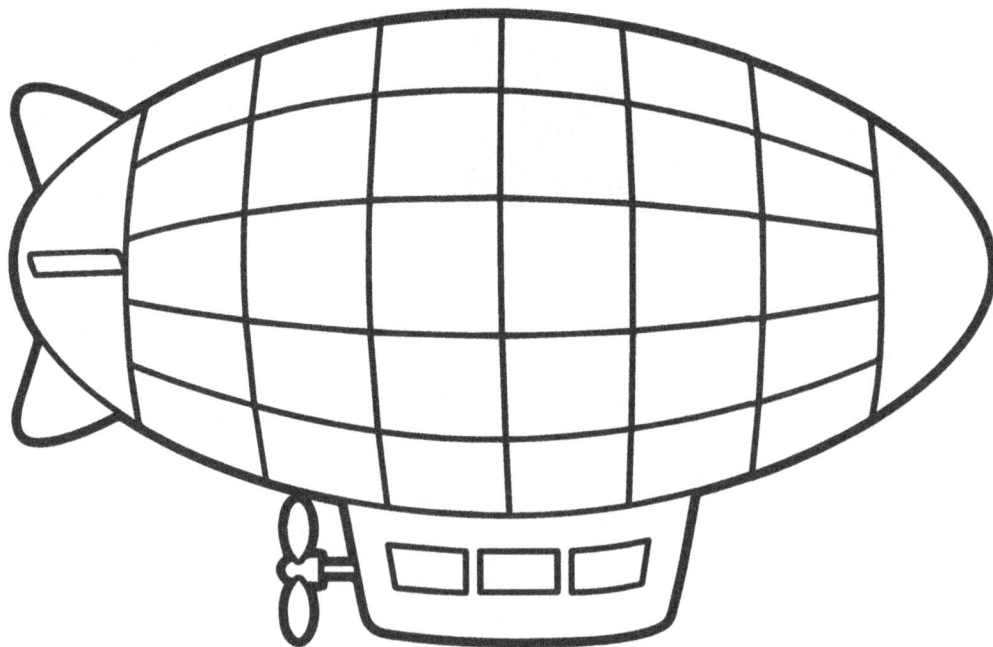

Made in the USA
Las Vegas, NV
14 August 2023